In the Darkest Time

I felt all alone,
Couldn't see what was in front of me,
but I knew I wanted to be free.

Looking at the universe so dark,
knowing through the darkness
there was light.

Ye are the light of the world. A city that is set on a hill cannot be hid. Neither do men light a candle and put it under a bushel, but on a candlestick; and it giveth light unto all that are in the house. Let your light shine before men, that they may see your good works, and glorify your father which is in heaven.

Matthew 5:14-16

In The Darkest
TIME
The
LIGHT
is GREATER

In The Darkest Time The Light is Greater
– Words of Love, Faith & Hope
Copyright © 2021 by Carolyn Williams

Scripture quotations marked "KJV" are taken from the King James Version of the Bible.

FIRST EDITION
Published in 2021

www.TheLightIsGreater.com

ISBN: 978-1-7367221-0-7

Library of Congress Control
Williams, Carolyn
In The Darkest Time The Light is Greater –Words of Love, Faith & Hope
Case Number: 1-10181555641 | February, 2021

Library of Congress in Publication Data
Category: Christian Poetry, Inspirational & Motivational
Written by: Carolyn Williams | carolynwilliams454@yahoo.com
Editing by: Tammy Bertron, Sue Malvagno, & Carolyn Williams
Design & Formatted by: Eli Blyden | www.EliTheBookGuy.com
Printed & Published in the United States | Tampa, Florida

To my mom, Lucille Williams Blash, who passed away September 12, 2000. My mother always told me: "Never give up on our dreams". Love and miss you so much.

~

To my family; Yolanda, Joseph, Jessica, Jacarlo, Ariyah, Rose and Maxine.

~

Also, to someone the Lord allowed to come into my life and heart, "GG" who passed in 2016.

Contents

In The
Darkest
TIME
The
LIGHT
is GREATER

Words of
Love, Faith & Hope

by Carolyn Williams

Introduction

Giving all the praise and honor to my heavenly Father, who gave me strength to keep going **IN THE DARKEST TIME** of my life, when it seemed as if things would never change no matter how I prayed. I had to **"Trust in the Lord with all my heart and lean not to my own understanding,"** and realize **He Is Greater than the Dark.**

In The Darkest Time The Light is Greater

Free Verse or Blank Verse Poems

You can let your thoughts run wild so that the words on the page read more like a conversation or story.

2020

We wanted 2019 to pass,
Never knowing 2020 would
Come in with such a blast.
Now looking at people wearing masks.

Standing 6 to 12 feet apart;
That's breaking our heart.
Many lives have been changed,
But nothing stays the same.

Our little ones can't understand.
Need to show them… things will be alright,
By washing their hands and wearing a mask.
That's how they can win this fight.

Corona – COVID-19 is what it's called;
It is trying to touch us all.
Everyone can take a stand,
And ruin Corona virus-COVID's plan.

There's more to the story;
Don't know where to begin.
Seems like we're living in a
World spinning within.

"I Can't Breathe," were the three words;
Wonder what the officer was thinking of!
We bend our knees to pray,
Not to take a life away!

Three words that changed the world,
"I Can't Breathe."
Again, what was he thinking of!
It surely wasn't love.

Now staring out our windows;
Trying to figure out
What is this march all about?
So many signs, it's blowing our mind.

Everyone needs to come together,
So the world can get better.
Loving one another is where to start.
"It comes from the heart."

We're in this together, because
In the Darkest Time The Light is Greater

Love

Your love was like sunshine
In the rain.
No matter how dark it was
You always brightened up the day.

I've seen smiles on your face…
There should have been tears.
Made me happy
Even if I felt sad.

I learned how to be a great Mom
By watching you.
Didn't call you Mom,
Called you Luc.
It's not the name that makes a Mom…

It is Love.

To my Mom, "Luc."
Thank you for being a wonderful Mom.

I Will See You at Heaven's Gate

Goodbye friend, whom I won't see again,
But wait! I will see you at Heaven's Gate!
Promise you I won't be late;
Waiting for my name to be called.

Holding on to all the memories inside
Of me no one sees.
The time we shared,
I will hold dear to my heart.
Goodbye friend,
I know it's not the end.

Until that day,
Can't wait to say hello again!
Promise you I won't be late.
I will see you at Heaven's Gate.

To my friend "GG"
who passed in 2016.

Taking the Mask Off

Every day I put on a mask
Pretending everything is ok.
Coming home, I take it off.
Now the real me comes out!

My family knows me;
Can't fool them.
See the hurt in their eyes
As I feel my voice rise.

My wife is scared to speak.
Once the mask comes off,
She never knows who she will meet.

Love at First Sight

The moment we saw them,
It was love at first sight.
Their tiny little body
Brings us so much delight.

Time to take them home,
We wrap them up to stay warm.
With sleepless nights and long hours,
It is still, love at first sight.

To new parents.

Captain

If it were not for the Captain
Who guides the ship of life,
I think I would have jumped off.

Tides and waves became so strong.
I ran to speak to the Captain.
He turned around; there stood Jesus.
My mind was at peace.

Tides and waves were still there,
But I knew my Captain
Would surely take me in safely.

Who's the Captain of your Ship?

I Still Hear You

You're not moving your lips;
I still hear you.
Even if your eyes don't have a tongue,
They can say something wrong.

In the silence of your voice…
You look the other way
Without saying a word,
I still hear you loud and clear.

Words don't have to be spoken
For a heart to be broken.

By Faith, Not by Sight

The sun may not shine;
Does it mean it's going to rain?
Cloudy skies don't always bring a storm.
We walk by faith, not by sight.

When our hope is gone and we feel all alone,
We walk by faith, not by sight,
The Lord is our eyes day and night.
We walk by faith, not by sight.

Sweetheart and Special Friend

At breakfast, for the last 50 years,
I have sat at our kitchen table
Gazing into your sparkling eyes.

My mind goes back in time remembering…
I couldn't wait for our first date and
Loving the way, you smile.

Seems like yesterday,
I spoke the first words,
"I love you."
Would do it all over again,
To have a sweetheart and special friend.

Heavenly Father

Heavenly Father, how I love You!
You are the Father who will
Always be there for me.

Each time my heart aches,
You are there to ease the pain.
In everything I do, You never change.
Your love remains the same.

Mom

Wow!
Where do these bright lights come from?
I want to go back,
But someone is pulling me out.
It was so dark and comfy inside,
Now the lights hurt my eyes.

Wait!
Being placed in someone's arms...
I recognize that voice!
Trying to see her face,
My head won't stay in place.

She is singing to me.
I remember that song!
It's My Mom!

To my granddaughter Jessica
who had her first baby girl 9/28/18.

His Promise

I saw a rainbow today.
It appeared after the rain.
A reminder of His promise
Not to destroy the world by sea.
His promise for everlasting life is:
He sent His son to die for you and me.

Love, Love

Love,
How do I find you?
I have a key to my door,
But when opening it,
Love doesn't welcome me anymore.

Once upon a time it brought me joy
When love opened the door.
It makes me sad now, because
Love no longer greets me at my door.

To Battered Women

Babies Having Babies

Babies having babies
Is what I hear everywhere I go.
Won't someone tell them to say "No!"

Young man over there,
She thought you really cared.
Being a father
Was more than you could bear.

Baby crying…
She doesn't know what to do,
For she's a baby, too;
Wants to play all day,
Now the baby takes her time away.

Loneliness, she feels all the time,
Thinking loving him would ease her mind.
Got to pay the price when you give life.
No one told her to say "No!"

Next time the young man says,
"Let me love you all night."
Tell him "No, that's not right!"
There are too many babies having babies.

Garden of Weeds

My garden of life was full of weeds.
Started out with one, then another.
Tried to pull them out,
They took control!
Wrapping me up,
My body and soul!

Wanted to get free,
Wouldn't let go of me.
How did they get there?

Weeds looking like flowers.
Trying to do things on my own
And not watching
What I brought home.
Soon finding myself with nothing left,
But weeds.

So overwhelmed,
I found a seed.
It was called
"The Word of Life."
I planted the word.
And all my weeds disappeared.

Thoughts

Satan comes after us
Because he knows our
Heavenly Father
Gave us free will.

Never expect the Father
To tell you what He's doing
In your life.
You have to trust Him.

When you are praying
To the Father,
Remember, it's a prayer,
Not a command.

Father waits every day to
Hear your prayers.
Have you talked to Him today?
If not, give him a prayer!

Life Is Like a Puzzle

Walking down the street with
Everything we own in our hands.
How did life get this way?
It wasn't the plan.

Thinking we have it all together,
Somehow what we thought
Doesn't matter.
Trying to figure life out,
It can be like a puzzle.
We have to find pieces that fit.

Sometimes we don't know how
The puzzle will look until it's finished.
Life can be that way, too.
When some of the pieces
Are put in place,
It doesn't always look like the cover.

Never Alone

Remember these words,
"You don't have to walk alone."
I know of a man who was born
To set you free.

In your time of need,
He's always there.
We may not see Him,
But Jesus really cares.
No one walks alone.

Our God knows you.
Some think He's too far,
But don't worry.
His love can reach you
No matter where you are.

Mother's Prayer

Oh, Father of Abraham, Isaac and Jacob,
I have seen Thy work in my life.
Coming on behalf of my children
Whom You knitted in my womb in the dark.

You are the God that looks on the inside.
Teach them how to seek You,
To look to You for their happiness.
Guide them to the promises
You have for them.

Make it so clear, the enemy can't
Deceive them with false hope.
It's a big world.
Keep their eyes on You,
For You hold the greatest promise… Everlasting life.

Inspired by the thoughts of a loving Mother "TB".

Waking Up

Waking up in the morning,
Feeling so fresh and free,
I speak to my Lord and
He speaks to me.

Washing my face,
Still feel His presence.
Combing my hair,
Never fearing He's not there.

Getting dressed and preparing
To leave the house.
I must put on more than clothes,
For if I don't,
Satan will try to take control.

So, I need to:

*"Put on the whole armor of God, that ye may be able
to stand against the wiles of the devil.
For we wrestle not against flesh and blood, but against
principalities, against power, against the rulers of the
darkness of this world, against spiritual wickedness in
high places.
Wherefore take unto you the whole armor of God, that*

ye may be able to withstand in the evil day, and having done all, to stand.

Stand therefore, having your loins girt about with truth, and having on the breastplate of righteousness; And your feet shod with the preparation of the gospel of peace.

Above all, taking the shield of faith, wherewith ye shall be able to quench all the fiery darts of the wicked.

And take the helmet of salvation, and the sword of the Spirit, which is the word of God:

Ephesians 6:11-17

Trade Shoes

I'm just a little kid trying to go to school.

Won't you play with me?
Will you be my friend?
Can I sit at your table?

Trade shoes with me just for a while;
See how I feel.
Maybe you will stop!

Do you think I look different than you?
What makes you feel this way?
Give me a chance to be your friend?

Trade shoes with me for a while
See how I feel.
Maybe you will stop!

You will see how it feels to sit all alone...
There's room at your table for more.
They are laughing at me
Going out the door.

Trade shoes with me just for a while;
See how I feel.
Maybe you will stop!

Be My Friend?

Don't Give Up

Your world may be spinning,
Can't get off.
Don't Give Up!
Jesus already won on the cross.

I know things don't look right,
Give it a try;
You don't have to die.
Tomorrow can change everything.
Don't Give Up!

It's up to you, no one else.
God loves you!
The choice is yours...
Don't Give Up!

To those who think life will never change.

Christmas In Heaven

One night before Christmas all through heaven,
It was so quiet not even the angels were singing,
Eyes were looking down on earth,
For the coming of the baby.

Father waiting to see
His only begotten Son born.
He called the angels to get ready
To announce the coming of His baby boy!

Now the time has come.
Heaven gave out a shout
With a multitude of
Angels praising God!

All looked down at the newborn King;
Heaven already knew His name;
A name that would be known
Throughout the world:
Jesus Christ, Emmanuel.

The Birth

The story was told,
His mother and earthly father
Couldn't find a place for Him
At the inn.

That little baby laying in a manger
Who couldn't find a place to be born;
Now sits in heaven on His throne
Where He belongs.

Things have changed;
He's no longer a baby,
He's our Savior!

Who Is She?

She brought me home,
Changed my diapers,
Made sure I was warm,
Cried and she held me
Close to her heart.

I saw her more as time went on,
Knew she was special.
Started to walk and she held my hand.
Spoke words to help me understand.

I'm off to college looking back
Through the years.
She changed my diaper,
Made sure I was warm.
And when crying,
She held me close to her heart.
Who is she?
The one who loves me.

To foster and adoptive parents.

Tick Tock

Tick tock, tick tock
That's what I hear.
The clock never moves,
But how time does fly!

My

My heart goes out to You.
My love overflows each time
I hear Your name.
My eyes wait for Your return.
My King of Kings,
My Lord of Lords.

A Tear

One day I felt a tear
Fall from my eyes,
Then I felt a gentle hand brushing
My tears away saying, "I promise you
There will be better days."
Thank You, Jesus.

First Love

You are my first love.
I will never stop loving You.
When I'm old and gray,
My love will never fade away.

I'm your bride waiting for Your return.
My heart belongs to You,
Will always be true,
So glad I said, "I do."

The family I have, You gave them to me.
A husband that is so special,
Two kids whom I love,
But You will always be my first love…
Jesus!

To my friend, Tammy, who loves Jesus.

Bird I Call Paradise

Come fly with me on a
Bird I call Paradise
To a place where
No one has gone before,
In a land of beauty
Where only love can live.

Paradise, come take me away.
My Paradise, let me ride on your
Wings in the wind of freedom.

Leaning back on your beautiful white back
Seeing the sun set like a marble in the sky.
Come fly with me on a bird I call Paradise.

Our King

Jesus wasn't wearing His crown the first time.
Came down in so much pain…
People thought He was the blame.
Was placed on a cross.
Wasn't the lamb that had to be caught,
Jesus gave up His life freely.

Running with The Wind

Let me run with the wind.
Seems like the wind is my only friend.
It says to me, *"Catch me if you can."*

It plays with my hair, blowing it in the air.
It tickles my ears, as it runs beside me
Saying, *"Catch me if you can."*

Sometimes I seem to win as I run
With the wind, but when I look again,
There goes my friend. Then I start
Running again and again.

I Know Who I Am!

The name they call me,
Is not really me, you see.
It won't let me be free.
I wake up in the morning
with the name they call me.

Sometimes I wonder why
I answer to that name?

For the name they call
Is not really me, you see.
My Lord and Savior has set me free
From the name they call me.

Our Dreams Are Near

Through the silence
We can hear
Our dreams are near.
Even in the dark
We can hear
Our dreams are near.
Our little light
That we hold is a reminder
Our dreams are good as gold.

Prayer Line: 247-7729

Picking up the phone
dialing 247-7729,
Always hearing a friendly voice
On the other line.

Helping me through the darkest time
And lonely night,
All was quiet, but not Christ.

Sometimes calling ten times a day;
Never turning me away.
Each voice sounding sweet;
Letting me know Jesus never sleeps.

Lord, thank You for 247-7729,
With so many friendly voices
On the other line.

To Mr. EIC
A face I 've never seen but a voice I'll never forget.
(Number is no longer in service)

I'm Going to Serve You

May not have tomorrow,
I do have today!
Going to live it by serving the Lord
And giving Him praise.

Trouble may come and trouble may go;
But I know it won't last forever.
Going to live for today,
Knowing God wants it this way.

Thank You, Lord,
Tomorrow is not promised to me,
But You have given me today.
I'm going to live it by serving You in every way.

Bring It On

Satan brings his people
To fight against you.
Tell him, "Come on!"

Bring them closer so you can tell
Them about Jesus.

He's the truth and light
That will set them free!

Hello World

What's wrong with this world today?
Don't they care what they hear
Or what they say?

Are you listening?
Give me an ear and I'll share
Something I hold so dear.

The love He has for you and me,
Is why Jesus shed His blood
So willingly.

Hand in Hand

Walking so far apart,
We forget the meaning of hand in hand.
Often feeling our color keeps us apart,
But we must learn to walk hand in hand.

Don't let our color stop us
From being sisters and brothers.
Same God that created you and me
Wants us to be free to love one another.

Great Pain Great Gain

My trials were hard,
But through every pain
There was gain.

My heart cried out.
Sometimes I was in doubt,
But through every pain,
There was gain.

I learned to listen,
I learned to obey,
I learned to do it God's way.

Hearing His voice meant so much.
Taught me how to stand in all my storms;
Making me strong.
Learning great pain, great gain.

Put Out A Hand

You never put out a hand;
Talked and talked about me,
Shoes were not new;
Had to wear them over and over,
But you never put out a hand.

My hurt you couldn't relate to;
Felt like you knew me,
But you never put out a hand.

I don't understand why.
I was waiting.
Saw my tears?
Oh no!   .
Because you weren't looking at me,
That's why you never put out a hand.

To the homeless.

What Do You Say?

Things don't go your way,
What do you say?
Wishing it was another day?
What do you say?

Do you stand there for a while?
Look and never smile?
What do you say?

This is what I say!
"The Lord will make a way."
I'm to stand and pray!

This Old House of Mine

Many years have passed,
This old house still stands.
Children have grown up with time.

My hair is gray;
My hands shake turning the door knob.

Friends, I see less, hellos are few.
Sitting on this old porch
Watching time take control.

I always say, "Thank you, Lord,
For blessing this old house of mine."

Someone Has to Care

We can shut our eyes
And pretend not to see.
We can close our hearts
To the love they need.

Why can't we understand?
Why must the children
Suffer so much?

Only to find out no one is there
To hear their cries,
Feed their empty stomachs.
Someone has to care.

To the broken-hearted.

Turn Around

When I was young, I asked everyone
If they loved me.
Went here and there,
Longing for someone to care.

If I had only turned around,
Would have seen Jesus's open arms
Reaching out to me.
I need only to turn around.

Satan Comes Without an Invitation

Jesus only comes
When we call upon Him,
Satan comes without an invitation.

He is the guest that is never welcome,
But always ready to invade your privacy.

Lifted Up

I'm falling,
Landing in the pit of hell.
When did it start, I couldn't tell.

Is that a Light I see?
Oh, please, let it be!

I'm being lifted up;
Whose hands do I feel?

The pit was dark;
Now I see Light!

Get Behind Me

My walk is not with you, Satan!
Get behind me.
Jesus has ordered my steps.
I am His and He is mine.
So, get behind me, where you belong.
My walk is not with you.

Teach Me

Lord, while I'm sleeping,
Give me peace.
Let me not take for granted
That I may wake in the morning,
Knowing it is You that gives me life.

Teach me how to use every moment
Serving You and others in all I do.
We're all Your children.

Give me a heart that can hear Your voice.
Show me how to love those
Who do not love me.

Direct me in the way I should go,
No matter if it's high or low.
I am the image of You.
Teach me.

Young, Black and Not So Bright

Young, black and not so bright" are only words to some people. To a lady I know, these words described her son. Time after time she asked for help, but it seemed like no one heard her cry... or no one really cared. This is not about color, but about the love a mother has for her son.

My son, what can I say?
Mama has tried in every way,
But it seems like no one cares.

They want to lock you up.
I love you so much!
What can I do, what can I say?

The birds are free to fly,
But you are about to die
With a life locked inside.

Maybe now he can be free like the birds. He killed himself playing "Russian Roulette" when he was 15.

Cleaning My Heart Out

A friend asked me,
"What are you doing?"
I said, "I'm cleaning my heart out."
"Cleaning your heart out?"

Making room for Jesus.
Told me He was coming today.
I want Him to stay
And never go away!

I'd rather have Jesus in my heart
More than anything.
I'm cleaning my heart out today.
I want Him to stay
And never go away!

No Fancy Wrapping Paper

I need, oh how I need, something
No one can take away.
Fancy wrapping paper I don't need.
Money doesn't matter, cause His love is free.
Jesus is the sweetest gift for me.

Tina's Letter

To whom it may concern:
Hi, my name is Tina.
May have seen me on the street,
And didn't know my name.
I'm the type you never want to meet.
When you see me, you walk on the other side.

Life at home wasn't good.
Didn't do what I should;
Was so misunderstood.
Going to bed, I was scared.
Couldn't call my mama,
She was nowhere to be found.
Cried all night, but no one cared.

The more I grew up, the more it hurt;
Pretty soon I felt like dirt.
Washing my body didn't make me feel clean.
Looked into the mirror and wondered,
Who is that staring back at me?
You see,
I never knew who Jesus wanted me to be!

*Thanks to the people at Created. There are so many faces
we see every day, never knowing their stories.*

Only One Time in Your Life

Only one time in your life
You come this way.
Only one time in your life
You have this day.

Let me hold your hand while I can,
Picking you up when you fall down.
Turning your frown around,
And putting a smile on your face.

I'm going to make it the best time of your life.
Going to rock you and hold you,
But most of all,
I'm going to love you.

It's the only time in your life
You come this way.

Written for my daughter Yolanda when she was born.

Good Night Prayer

Father God,
Please hear our prayer.
Watch over our family while we sleep.
Keep us safe and place an
Angel by our side.

We go to bed knowing
Nothing about tomorrow.
Believing You are guiding us.
As we arise give us peace.

One by one we go on our way
Put joy in our hearts and show us
Your love always.
Let Mercy and Grace follow us
Everywhere we go.

The Kiddy Song

I love Jesus and Jesus loves me.
It's the greatest love
You will ever see.

It's the kind of love
That needs no money.
It's the kind of love
That needs no looks.
It's the kind of love
That will get you hooked.

He's the bee in my bonnet
That keeps me right.
He tells me, "I love you" every night.
I say to Him, "I love You right back."

I love Jesus and Jesus loves me.
It's the greatest love
You will ever see.
Cause I love Jesus and
Jesus loves me.

Stop

Smell the roses once in a while,
That's how Jesus stays on our mind.
Stop and see the beauty of the flowers,
That have so many colors.

Look at the grass, it grows so green,
With just a little water
And not too much bother.

Your work is so beautiful.
I sit and look in amazement at how
It must have been in the Garden of Eden.
This is Your world,
Lord God!

Family

Everyone hurrying to start the day,
Rushing to get on our way.
But, we don't forget to pray.

The dog and cat trying to get out.
Dad doing his best not to shout.
Love is what the family is all about.

Spending time together is what we do.
Before we know it, time has passed
And we will say, "That was fast."

Let's enjoy one another while we can.
The family is God's plan.
Holding every precious moment
Close to our heart,
Because the family is the most important part.

To families, "The most Important Part."

Material Things

Material things I don't need.
Possessions don't come first in my life;
They only last a short time.

Some things can be taken away
Or broken into little pieces
By holding on too tightly.

Material things are not here to stay,
But, His love will never fade away.
Jesus's love lasts forever.

Look Up!

Why do you go around
Always looking down?

Don't you know Jesus died
On the cross to set you free?
He loves both you and me.

When this world tells you
"You're not going to make it,"
Are you just going to
Sit there and take it?
Look up!

Believe in Jesus

Believe in Jesus, and He will set you free.
Walk in the steps He prepares for you.
You may be afraid,
But never fear, He will be near.

Love is what He is made of,
Faith will guide you all the way.
Hope is all you need…
Believe in Jesus.

Jesus Loves You

Always remember,
Keep a song in your heart
No matter where you go.
It'll keep you on your way;
Put a song in your heart and pray.

Keep a smile on your face,
And He will give you grace,
Because no one can take His place.
Jesus loves you.

Patience

Kids, our love,
The ones who tug on our apron string
While time is getting late.
Seems like we can't get a break!

Time for bed,
They want to play,
Leaving us shaking our head.

Waking up in the morning,
Ready to play in the snow.

One day they will be grown,
With kids of their own.

We won't need patience anymore…
He will be knocking on their door.

He is the Potter and I Am the Clay

God knows me,
He doesn't see what the world sees,
For He is the Potter and I am the clay.

In my storms, when everything
Is blowing out of place,
I don't worry, because
He is the Potter and I am the clay.

Special Baby

God said, I have a special baby
That needs a special family.
He looked down on earth…
"There they are."

He gave the baby a kiss.
"Don't you worry,
I know their hearts.
They will love you… no matter who you are."

The seed was planted.
Then one day it happened… a little bump!
Your prayer has been answered.

Nine months is over and baby is here,
…Something is wrong.
Someone said, "He can't hear."
Doctor, what's going to happen?

"At one–he will not walk,
Three–might not see,
Six–all he will do is sit.
I'm sorry this happened to you."

When everything is said and done
…You are still our son.
The Lord gave you to us…
God wanted someone He could trust
With His special baby…
Whom He loves so much.

To all the special babies.

Author's Note

I would like to share with you my caring verse the Lord gave to me many years ago. There were times when I thought He had forgotten about me, but somehow this verse would find me, not me find it. I soon realized He was assuring me that **He would do what He said.**

I will instruct thee and teach thee in the way which thou shalt go: I will guide thee with mine eye.

Psalm 32:8

These words are so true. Whatever path you may walk, He will:

- Instruct — When you instruct someone, you're giving them a set of tools to do something specific.
- Teach — to give someone knowledge or to train someone.
- Guide — to assist (a person); to travel through or reach a destination or unfamiliar area, as by accompanying or giving directions to the person.

He instructs, teaches and guides us with His eye. Guiding us with His eye. That means He is always there and we are never alone. Have you ever seen a greater love than this?

It's also Good to Remember:

*Be ye not as the horse, or as the mule, which have no
understanding: whose mouth must be held in with bit
and bridle, lest they come near unto thee.*

Psalm 32:9

God bless you for reading
In The Darkest Time The Light is Greater
and may you find
The Light in Your Darkest Time.

In The Darkest Time The Light is Greater

Acknowledgements

Thanking all of my friends who shared so much of their time to help me.

Tammy and Stewart, thank you. I came into your home in 1999. Tammy, you showed me how to believe in myself...with action. Truly, without your help, this could have not happened. Mr. Stewart (he always tells me to call him Stewart!), you walk and talk softly, but have a big heart for people. I'm so happy you like the book - it means so much to me.

Sue, you contributed so much to the book! You typed it, while dealing with tragedy in your family. Thank you from the bottom of my heart.

Tom, you have been such a blessing in my life. Thank you for the Godly words you spoke and being a vessel to me.

Marlene, my Marlene, you're a tough cookie. Thank you for your honesty. *Mr. Harry,* you're no longer with us, but you encouraged me in my writing.

Grace, you were a light in my darkest time. I value your closeness with the Lord and am so blessed that I can call upon you when I need help.

Thanks to **Kenneth and Gladys,** who work at Fresh Market. You will never know the joy you brought to me with your kind words.

Doreen, your spirit is such a peaceful blessing.

Chris and *Mary Lou,* my two best friends. You have seen me and my family in our darkest time. I thank God for both of you.

Kim, thank you for sharing your ideas with me.

Made in the USA
Columbia, SC
17 June 2021